EXPLORING CIVIL RIGHTS

THE MOVEMENT
1965

JAY LESLIE

Franklin Watts®
An imprint of Scholastic Inc.

Content Consultants

Senator Nan Grogan Orrock
State of Georgia

Crystal R. Sanders, Ph.D.
Associate Professor of History
Pennsylvania State University

Library of Congress Cataloging-in-Publication Data
Names: Leslie, Jay, author.
Title: Exploring civil rights— the movement : 1965 / by Jay Leslie.
Description: First edition. | New York : Franklin Watts, an imprint of Scholastic Inc., [2022] | Series: Exploring civil rights | Includes bibliographical references and index. | Audience: Ages 10–14. | Audience: Grades 5–8.
Identifiers: LCCN 2021020377 (print) | LCCN 2021020378 (ebook) | ISBN 9781338769838 (library binding) | ISBN 9781338769845 (paperback) | ISBN 9781338769852 (ebook)
Subjects: LCSH: African Americans—Civil rights—History—Juvenile literature. | Civil rights movements—United States—History—20th century—Juvenile literature. | Civil rights workers—United States—Juvenile literature. | BISAC: JUVENILE NONFICTION / History / United States / 20th Century | JUVENILE NONFICTION / History / United States / General
Classification: LCC E185.615 .L47 2022 (print) | LCC E185.615 (ebook) | DDC 323.1196/073—dc23
LC record available at https://lccn.loc.gov/2021020377
LC ebook record available at https://lccn.loc.gov/2021020378

10 9 8 7 6 5 4 3 2 1   22 23 24 25 26

Printed in Heshan, China 62
First edition, 2022

ON THE COVER: In 1965, protesters march along a 54-mile-long route from Selma to Montgomery, Alabama.

Series produced by 22MediaWorks, Inc.
President LARY ROSENBLATT
Book design by FABIA WARGIN and AMELIA LEON
Editor SUSAN ELKIN
Copy Editor LAURIE LIEB
Fact Checker BRETTE SEMBER
Photo Researcher DAVID PAUL PRODUCTIONS

PREVIOUS PAGE: Demonstrators lock arms in front of the Dallas County courthouse in Selma, Alabama.

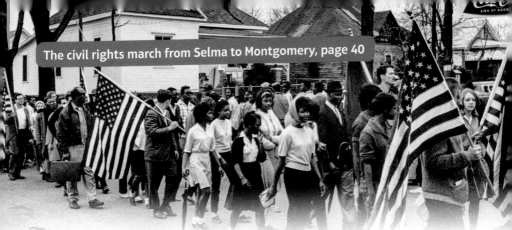

The civil rights march from Selma to Montgomery, page 40

Table of Contents

Malcolm X, page 18

A **Ku Klux Klan** member is dressed in a white hood and robe to hide his identity during a parade in 1924.

The Way It Was

In December 1865, the Thirteenth Amendment to
the U.S. Constitution abolished slavery in the United
States. By the early 1870s, former slaveholding states
in the South created Black codes to strictly limit the
freedom of their Black citizens. These restrictions were
known as "**Jim Crow**" laws, and they controlled where
people who used to be enslaved could live and work.

Jim Crow laws were expanded in the 1880s to
keep Black citizens from voting or receiving a proper
education. In many parts of the South, they were
forced to use separate restaurants, schools, restrooms,
parks, and other public places. This practice is known
as **segregation**. Although laws said that these spaces
should be "separate but equal," facilities for Black
people were almost always inferior to those assigned
to white citizens.

It was not uncommon for Black citizens in the
South to be kidnapped and beaten, shot, or killed for
small violations of Jim Crow laws. **Lynchings** and
white mob violence frequently terrorized many
Black communities. Black churches were burned

down, and Black homes attacked. **Discrimination** against Black Americans also existed in the North and elsewhere in the nation, but less so than in the South at the time.

Fighting Back

Segregation, Jim Crow laws, and discrimination denied Black Americans the same **civil rights** as white Americans. In the face of **oppression** and terror, some Black Americans organized to fight inequality. The first civil rights organization in the United States was founded in 1896 as the National Association of Colored Women's Clubs. In 1909, an interracial group of **activists** formed the National Association for the Advancement of Colored People (NAACP). The NAACP called for an end to segregation in schools, public transportation, and other areas of daily life. The group also focused on making the American public aware of the violence against Black people.

In the following years, new civil rights groups emerged. Christian ministers, African American lawyers, and Black youth were especially important in organizing and supporting the emerging civil rights movement. The decade between 1955 and 1965 would serve as the heart of the movement, as action and long awaited progress began to take shape.

Protesters carrying a banner that says "We march with Selma!" lead 15,000 people in a march through Harlem in New York City on March 15, 1965.

1965

In this book, you'll see how in 1965, the civil rights movement was going strong. But a century of racism could not be undone overnight. Even after 10 years into the movement, the fight for true equality was far from over. You'll learn how Malcolm X became an influential figure, and how his **assassination** impacted the movement. You'll learn how demonstrators pushed for Black voting rights along the historic Selma to Montgomery March, remaining peaceful in the face of brutal police officers. And you'll see how, because of that march, the **federal** government passed the Voting Rights Act of 1965, finally empowering Black citizens to have a say in the leadership of their own communities. ∎

Young activists sing and chant during a demonstration for voter rights at the courthouse in Selma, Alabama, in February 1965. More than 400 of them were arrested and jailed.

1

Visions of a Great Society

While the Reverend Dr. Martin Luther King, Jr., might have been the face of the movement in 1965, it was thousands of ordinary Black Americans and their white allies who made the movement possible.

Five years earlier, an interracial group of students had united to form the Student Nonviolent Coordinating Committee (SNCC). Their mission was to build on the activism inspired by sit-ins across the country, and to give young people a voice in the movement. On January 2, 1965, SNCC leaders announced to the nation where they would focus their protest efforts next: Alabama. In Selma, only a small percentage of eligible Black voters had actually been able to register. That wasn't for a lack of trying. African Americans in Selma, within Dallas County, *wanted* to register. They wanted to vote.

Voter Suppression

Although white residents were a minority in Dallas County, they had a clear majority in the local government—and they wanted to keep it that way. So the politicians in charge did whatever they could to keep African Americans from voting. This is known as **voter suppression**. They established **poll taxes**, requiring Black voters to pay a large sum of money before registering.

They also devised "literacy tests" that claimed to measure whether someone could read. In reality, white examiners often rigged the tests with impossible questions to answer. One Black man was asked, "How many bubbles are in a bar of soap?"

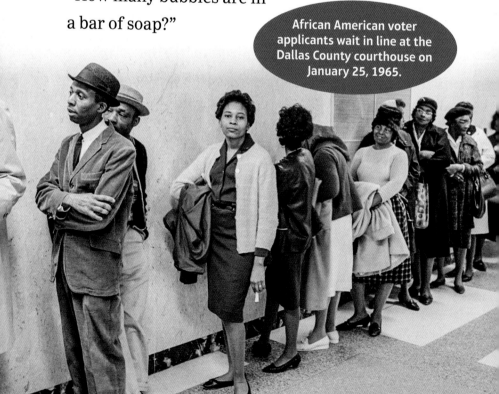

African American voter applicants wait in line at the Dallas County courthouse on January 25, 1965.

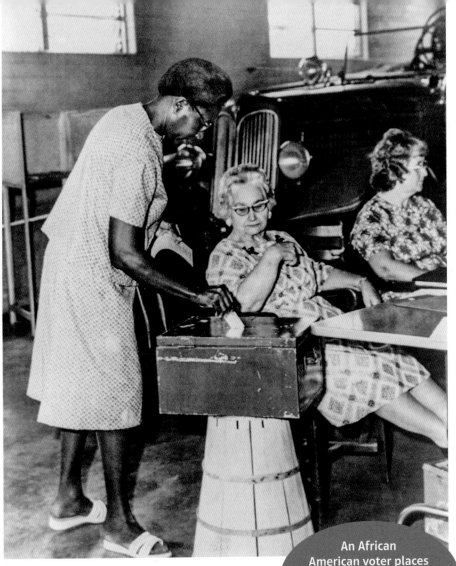

An African American voter places her ballot in a box during an election in Jackson, Mississippi.

And if tests didn't work, then white residents would resort to outright intimidation and violence.

SNCC would start by empowering eligible voters in Alabama. They vowed that Black Americans in Dallas County would soon have the right to vote—and if SNCC could bring voting rights to Dallas County, it could bring them to the entire United States.

President Lyndon B. Johnson (center) delivers the State of the Union address in the U.S. Capitol on January 4, 1965. This is the first State of the Union ever broadcast on TV during prime time.

A Great Society

On January 4, 1965, two days after SNCC's announcement, President Lyndon B. Johnson delivered his State of the Union address. A few months earlier, Johnson had signed the Civil Rights Act of 1964 into law. Across America, millions of people of all races tuned in to hear if his words to the nation would address discrimination and equal rights.

Johnson announced his bold vision: to transform America into a "great society." His Great Society initiative would create job opportunities that allowed people to better their quality of life, and it would provide quality public education for all children. In a great society, no American, regardless of race, would be left behind. Johnson promised 1965 would be a year of real change.

American Football League All-Star Game

On January 10, twenty-one Black players of the American Football League refused to play in the league's All-Star game, which was to be held in New Orleans, Louisiana, later that week. From the moment they had arrived in the city, they'd experienced extreme racism—club owners closed their doors to Black players, taxi drivers denied them service, and people hurled insults everywhere they turned. The players protested this racist behavior until the game was eventually relocated to Houston, Texas.

Some white players on the All-Star team joined the Black players' boycott to pressure the league to move the game out of New Orleans.

Freedom Day

Encouraged by President Johnson's commitment to equality, SNCC jumped into action on its plans for Dallas County. It targeted the city of Selma, Alabama, where 57 percent of the population was Black, but only *2 percent* of Black adults had been able to register to vote. Dr. King and the Southern Christian Leadership Conference (SCLC) joined SNCC in this campaign.

On January 18, 1965, declaring "Today Is Freedom Day," King and John Lewis, the chair of SNCC, gathered 300 Black voters at the Brown Chapel AME

A long line of African Americans await their turn to enter the courthouse in Selma, Alabama, in an effort to register to vote.

Church in Selma. The group marched peacefully to the courthouse to register to vote. At least, that was the plan.

When the group reached the front doors of the courthouse, Sheriff Jim Clark shook his head. "You wait back there." He pointed to the cramped alley behind the courthouse. The marchers waited patiently for hours, but courthouse officials never called them inside. The office closed without allowing a single person to register.

"Don't be disheartened," King told the crowd. "We'll come back tomorrow."

On January 22, 1965, Dallas County sheriff James G. Clark prods a teacher in the back in an aggressive attempt to prevent African American teachers from registering to vote.

Teachers' March

Black teachers could be fired for participating in demonstrations, so many hesitated to join the civil rights movement. On January 22, 1965, however, the teachers in Selma had had enough. More than one hundred educators—nearly every Black teacher in the city— marched together to register to vote. Sheriff Clark's deputies shoved them down the courthouse stairs three times, but the teachers persisted. In the end, they were not arrested, but they were unable to register.

When the marchers did return the next day, however, they were told that the registration office was closed. But this time, the crowd decided to enter the courthouse anyway, through the front door, like Selma's white citizens.

Within moments, outraged police swarmed and arrested every single person who was with Dr. King, herding the crowd with cattle prods. They dragged an eight-year-old girl to jail in handcuffs. Sixty people were charged with crimes that day.

Even though protesters were met with police violence, King maintained a policy of nonviolence, urging everyone standing by his side to remain peaceful. ∎

Sheriff Clark shoves Amelia Boynton as other Black Americans line up at the courthouse to try to register to vote.

Malcolm X, an African American minister and political activist, in 1964.

2

Malcolm X

SNCC, Martin Luther King, Jr., and his supporters had committed to **nonviolent resistance** for the past ten years of the civil rights movement. Police shot at demonstrators. Segregationists bombed their houses. But the peaceful activists believed they should not fight back against their attackers.

One prominent civil rights leader, however, a man named Malcolm X, did not agree with this approach. Malcolm X believed that self-defense was a human right. Black people should be able to defend themselves, their families, and their communities when attacked.

Malcolm X also thought that King and his supporters were embarrassing themselves by insisting on **integration**, as if they were begging white people for permission to participate in institutions that did not want them. Instead, Malcolm X envisioned a world where oppressed

Black Americans could create their own communities, where they would live and thrive separately from racist white institutions.

By 1965, these ideas had gained Malcolm X thousands of followers not only in the United States, but also in Black communities around the world.

A Boy with No Future

He may have been a prominent leader in the 1960s, but when he was a child, no one expected Malcolm X—who was born Malcolm Little—to amount to much.

Malcolm grew up in Lansing, Michigan, where he and his family suffered attacks at the hands of **white supremacist** hate groups. Malcolm dreamed of making real change. "I'm going to be a lawyer," he told his white teacher when he was sixteen. But his teacher just laughed, "That's no realistic goal for a Negro."

Police mugshot of Malcolm Little, later known as Malcolm X.

Malcolm Little spent part of his sentence at the Charlestown Prison in Massachusetts.

Crushed and ashamed, Malcolm dropped out of school. He felt like he had no future. He began to get into trouble and in 1946, at age 20, he was sent to prison for burglary.

Black Pride

While serving his sentence, Malcolm found out that his brother Reginald had joined an all-Black religious group called the **Nation of Islam**. His brother wrote to Malcolm that Black people shouldn't be ashamed of their skin color. In fact, they should be *proud*.

In a world where African Americans were spat on, beaten, arrested, shot, and even lynched for being Black, being proud was not a common idea. It filled Malcolm with strength and a sense of purpose. He joined the Nation of Islam while he was still in prison.

Elijah Muhammad (right), founder and head of the Nation of Islam, stands at a podium in Chicago to introduce Malcolm X (center) in February 1961.

A New Revolutionary

One of Malcolm's first symbolic acts as a member of the Nation of Islam was to change his last name. He learned that "Little" had been passed down from slave owners, because masters gave their own last names to their slaves. He had no way of knowing the true names of his African ancestors who had been kidnapped by slave traders and sold into slavery. So he changed his last name simply to "X," casting off what he called his slave name.

Upon his release from prison, Malcolm X set to work helping other African Americans break free of the shame that racism had forced on them. He became a minister and, preaching freedom and **liberation**, soon increased the membership of the Nation of Islam from 500 to 30,000 across the country.

People packed tightly into halls and temples just to hear his fiery speeches. For many African Americans, this was the first time that they'd ever heard that they were strong, that they could rely on themselves, that they didn't have to try to join white society but could create their own communities free of racism and oppression. Malcolm X called this idea Black separatism.

Malcolm X addresses a crowd in Harlem in New York City in June 1963.

Malcolm X Makes Enemies

Malcolm X disagreed with Dr. King on many issues including the strategies of nonviolence and integration. He felt King wasn't radical enough. Rather than protests against segregation, Malcolm X called for building the resources and independence of the Black community through the Nation of Islam.

Malcolm's rising popularity often was seen as a threat by other Black leaders. Elijah Muhammad, the founder of the Nation of Islam, became resentful as he realized that Malcolm X was gaining more followers than Muhammad ever had. Malcolm X broke away from the group in 1964 because of disagreements with Muhammad.

Black Muslims picket in front of the New York Criminal Courts Building, where two Nation of Islam members were to stand trial.

James Baldwin (left) and William F. Buckley (right).

Baldwin-Buckley Debate

James Baldwin was a Black poet, novelist, playwright, and essayist who spoke out against racism. He was also a close friend to both Malcolm X and Martin Luther King, Jr. In February 1965, Baldwin went head-to-head with the white conservative author William F. Buckley. At the University of Cambridge, before a large gathering, they debated the question "Has the American dream been achieved at the expense of the American Negro?" Buckley was convinced that racism no longer affected Black Americans, but Baldwin proved him wrong. When the audience voted for the winner of the debate, Baldwin won overwhelmingly, with 544 votes to 164.

In The Gambia, crowds celebrate Independence Day on February 18, 1965.

Global Black Liberation

While African Americans fought against oppression in the United States, other Black activists fought for their own rights all around the world. In February 1965, the African country of The Gambia gained independence from Britain, which had controlled it since 1821. Meanwhile, in South Africa, native Africans suffered under a legal system of segregation called **apartheid**. People across the entire African continent protested the ways that France, Britain, Spain, Belgium, and Portugal were exploiting their countries. Independence movements also ignited in the United Kingdom and in the Caribbean.

Malcolm X Finds a New Way Forward

After Malcolm X broke away from the Nation of Islam, he took his message of Black freedom overseas. He spoke with prominent leaders across Africa and the Middle East, calling for solidarity. The racial struggle in the United States was only a small part of a larger story about the oppression of Black people around the world.

He emphasized this when speaking to hundreds of students at the historically Black Tuskegee Institute in Alabama on February 3, 1965. The next day, he traveled to Selma to speak about the importance of Black **suffrage** at Brown Chapel AME Church. Although he had previously disagreed with the nonviolent methods of SCLC and SNCC, his trips to Africa encouraged him to stand in solidarity with *all* Black people. ∎

Malcolm X meets with Prince Faisal al-Saud, of Saudi Arabia, during a visit as a guest of state.

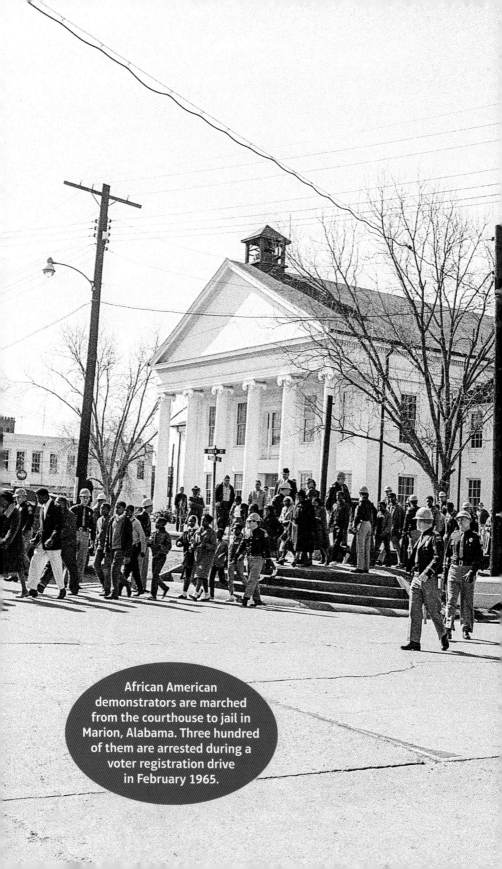

African American demonstrators are marched from the courthouse to jail in Marion, Alabama. Three hundred of them are arrested during a voter registration drive in February 1965.

3

A Peaceful Protest Turns Deadly

By the beginning of February 1965, SNCC and Dr. King had been working hard on the Selma voter registration campaign for more than a month. Yet they had little to show for their efforts. In that time, they'd managed to register just 100 new African American voters. However, in that same time frame, 3,000 campaign workers, Black residents, and activists had been arrested, and hundreds more had been injured, fired from their jobs, or both.

SNCC encouraged its supporters to stay hopeful. Leaders organized a peaceful demonstration on February 18, planning to sing hymns in front of the local county jail in Marion, Alabama, where police had locked up a civil rights worker.

In Jonathan Frost's mural *The Death of Jimmie Lee Jackson*, Jackson is pictured defending his mother in Marion, Alabama, in 1965.

In an effort to stop the protest, police became violent. The streetlights were turned off and police turned on the unarmed crowd.

Some in the crowd had run from police to a local diner nearby. Police followed and began beating the protesters. One young man named Jimmie Lee Jackson jumped in front of his mother to protect her. A state trooper shot him twice. As he bled out, a circle of other police officers beat him. He died eight days later. His death would be a turning point in the campaign in Selma.

On February 21, 1965, the civil rights movement suffered another major blow when Malcolm X was assassinated. That afternoon, an eager crowd of 400

The Autobiography of Malcolm X

At the time of Malcolm X's assassination, writer Alex Haley had been hard at work on *The Autobiography of Malcolm X*. Haley had written it based on interviews he'd had with the revolutionary leader over the past two years. However, in response to the assassination, the publisher immediately announced that it would no longer publish the book due to the controversy surrounding Malcolm's death. Haley refused to give up on the manuscript. Thirteen publishing houses rejected it before he finally convinced one, Grove Press, to take on the project, and the monumental auto-biography hit the shelves later that year. Over the past six decades, this powerful book continues to influence readers and activists around the world.

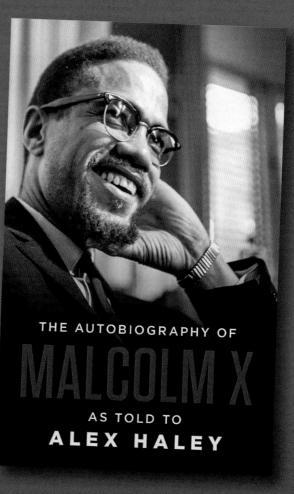

THE AUTOBIOGRAPHY OF

MALCOLM X

AS TOLD TO

ALEX HALEY

The Autobiography of Malcolm X has sold five million copies since its publication in 1965.

people gathered in the Audubon Ballroom in New York City to hear Malcolm X speak. As he took the stage, the crowd fell silent. Suddenly, three gunmen sprang up from the audience and started shooting.

Malcolm X collapsed on stage. By the time police arrived, he'd been shot 21 times. He was pronounced dead shortly after. The police eventually arrested three members of the Nation of Islam, who were found guilty of the assassination. However, questions still remain about the real motivations behind the murder.

Followers of Malcolm X kneel by the mortally wounded Black Muslim leader on February 21, 1965.

Planning the Selma to Montgomery March

On March 3, the African Americans in Selma gathered to mourn the tragic murder of Jimmie Lee Jackson. Malcolm X's assassination was also fresh on their minds.

At the funeral service, King's words reminded the mourners who prayed around the coffin that Jackson's death should not be in vain.

James Bevel, the director of the SCLC's voter registration campaign in Selma, proposed a nonviolent march from Selma to Montgomery, the capital of Alabama, on March 7. The march would

The Reverend James Bevel proposed and organized the Selma to Montgomery march.

symbolize the long road to equality. Along the way, marchers would call for the voting rights that Jimmie Lee Jackson had lost his life for.

The 54-mile stretch would take several days to travel. In order to leave Selma, participants would have to cross the Edmund Pettus Bridge, at the edge of the city. They knew that countless segregationists, white supremacists, and Ku Klux Klan members would attack them along the way. Alabama Governor George Wallace vowed to stop the march at all costs.

President Johnson's Second Act

Activists in Selma weren't the only ones concerned with Black suffrage, or the right to vote, in the Deep South. King brought the matter to President Lyndon B. Johnson's attention during a meeting on March 5, prompting the president to monitor the situation with growing concern. The Civil Rights Act of 1964 was supposed to protect the rights of all people, but King explained that it hadn't gone far enough.

Johnson planned to pass another act to grant the federal government the power to run elections and register African Americans to vote in the southern states. And he needed to pass this bill as quickly as possible.

President Johnson and Dr. King discuss the Voting Rights bill in March 1965, before it passed in Congress.

Johnson's political advisers, however, had other ideas. The first civil rights bill had become law just a few months earlier. Johnson's advisers argued that passing more **legislation** so quickly might make white voters uncomfortable, causing Johnson to lose the next election.

Johnson weighed his advisers' words carefully. Ultimately, he agreed with them and backed down. Justice in Selma would have to wait.

Bloody Sunday

On March 7, activists in Selma began the first march toward Montgomery. The march was led by civil rights leaders John Lewis and Hosea Williams.

Hosea Williams and John Lewis lead marchers across the Edmund Pettus Bridge in Selma, Alabama, on Bloody Sunday.

PETTUS BRIDGE

SNCC leader John Lewis (light coat, center) attempts to protect himself as a state trooper swings his club at Lewis's head.

Dr. King gave his support, but he did not attend, which made SNCC hesitant; it would be harder to gain public support without King marching at the front. Six hundred marchers, most of them from the area around Selma, gathered along U.S. Highway 80. They were nervous. Some prayed and held hands.

Sheriff Jim Clark was prepared for the march. That morning, he called all white men in Selma over the age of 21 to come to the courthouse to be **deputized**. This meant that they had the force of the law behind them.

Clark did not let the marchers get far. Before they had even finished crossing the Edmund Pettus Bridge, the men were ordered to charge. Police galloped through the crowd on horseback. They swung night-sticks. They sprayed tear gas, blinding the marchers and clouding the bridge in a chemical haze.

That day, dozens of marchers suffered injuries in what came to be known as Bloody Sunday. News stations around the country interrupted normal programming to broadcast images from the brutal attacks on men, women, and children who refused to fight back. The blatant violence shocked white Americans. But the marchers would not be deterred.

The Second March to Montgomery

On March 9, 1965, two days after the first failed attempt, SNCC and SCLC led another march across the Edmund Pettus Bridge. This time, King stood at the front, and 2,000 clergy members and Black and white citizens from all over the country traveled to Selma to stand by his side.

SNCC requested a court order from a U.S. District Court judge to ban the state from stopping the march. Instead the judge issued a temporary restraining order directing the protesters to postpone the march.

King decided to lead the march as planned. However, once the crowd reached the bridge, he stopped, led the group in prayer, and then turned around to lead them back the way they had come. He had decided to obey the restraining order to prove to the rest of the country that the Black activists were good citizens.

That night, KKK members attacked three white ministers who had come to join the demonstration.

A long line of marchers pray on the highway near Selma on March 9, 1965.

One of the ministers, James Reeb, died from his injuries. His death received widespread news coverage, and tens of thousands of people across the country held vigils in his memory. Nationwide support for the marchers grew. In the face of growing public support for legislation, President Johnson promised to draft a voting rights bill immediately. The bill landed in Congress on March 17.

The Third March to Montgomery

The first and second marches had both ended in defeat. But on March 21, King tried again. This time, 8,000 people joined him in Selma. He received a federal court order permitting the march, and the

Black and white participants persevere along the five-day, 54-mile civil rights march from Selma to Montgomery, Alabama, in March 1965.

National Guard and the U.S. Army were called in for protection. The marchers also took heart in the fact that the voting rights bill had reached Congress just a few days earlier. But the fight wasn't over yet.

By the time marchers reached Montgomery, their numbers had swelled to more than three times the original number: 25,000 triumphant people reached the Montgomery courthouse on March 25.

Inspired by the march, volunteers from all over the country drove to Alabama to work in voter registration drives. Congress was still locked in the long process of debating the Voting Rights bill, but in the meantime volunteers were determined to solve voter suppression themselves. ■

While guards continue to conduct tours, young activists sit in around the Liberty Bell in Philadelphia's Independence Hall.

4

Going to War against the War

The Selma march was a victory, but protesters could not afford to stop fighting, even for a day. As Congress debated the Voting Rights bill for months, several activists shifted their focus to protesting anti-Black violence and hate crimes.

All over the country, African Americans were often beaten in the streets, and police just turned a blind eye—or participated in the beatings themselves. Enraged by the violence he'd seen happening in Selma, a young African American named Michael Simmons organized 3,000 students to march through his hometown of Philadelphia, Pennsylvania, in the spring of 1965. The peaceful march called for both the federal and state government to take action against anti-Black violence.

A crowd of women, including Jeannette Rankin (center with glasses), the first woman elected to Congress, protest the Vietnam War outside Union Station in Washington, DC, in 1965.

Taking a Stand against Vietnam

On April 1 and 2, 1965, the SCLC convened to discuss where it should focus its activist efforts next. Dr. King wanted the organization to take a stand publicly opposing the war in Vietnam.

The United States was caught in the middle of a bloody war against North Vietnam. That year, 1,928 American soldiers would die in combat. Forty percent of those Americans were Black and many were poor. While upper- and middle-class white citizens could join the Army Reserve and National Guard to avoid being sent to Vietnam, Black Americans did not have the same option. Racial discrimination prevented most Black men from being allowed to join. Both the Army Reserve and the National Guard were extremely selective. Their members were often able to avoid combat postings in Vietnam.

The Vietnam War

In 1954, the Southeast Asian country of Vietnam split into two separate governments, North Vietnam and South Vietnam. North Vietnam wanted the country to be governed by **communism**, while the South did not. With support from the Soviet Union, North Vietnam made strides to take over South Vietnam, resulting in war. Fears that communism would spread around the globe led the United States to officially enter the war in 1964. The U.S. role in Vietnam would not end until 1973, and its involvement was considered a failure by many Americans. Fifty-eight thousand U.S. soldiers died in battle, and the South eventually fell to communist rule. The North and the South were united to become the Socialist Republic of Vietnam.

U.S. soldiers on patrol in Vietnam in 1965.

However, racial discrimination prevented Black men from being chosen for these desired postings.

King's passionate call to action that day, however, was met with silence. Many felt protesting the war would feel like a betrayal to Johnson. They were worried about undoing all the progress they had just made in the South.

Education Reform

While the SCLC debated Johnson's approach to the war, the president began the next phase of his Great Society program. He started focusing on education.

On April 11, the federal government passed the Elementary and Secondary Education Act of 1965. This guaranteed much-needed financial aid to

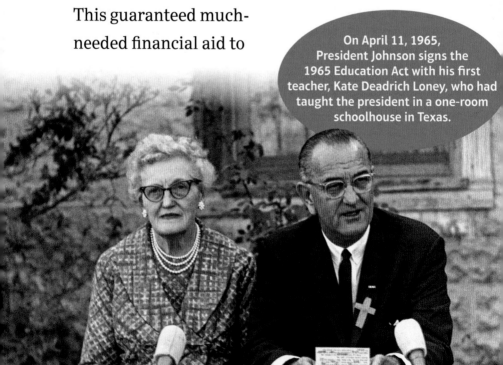

On April 11, 1965, President Johnson signs the 1965 Education Act with his first teacher, Kate Deadrich Loney, who had taught the president in a one-room schoolhouse in Texas.

As part of President Johnson's Great Society programs, the first lady, Lady Bird Johnson, reads to children in a Project Head Start classroom in Washington, DC.

public schools—especially schools that served a high percentage of **low-income**, mostly Black students.

For too long, income had determined education in the United States. High-income families could afford to live in areas with excellent school systems, while children from low-income families were crowded into underfunded schools with underpaid teachers. The new law aimed to give everyone the same opportunities.

This act also permanently established a program called Head Start. The program provided education, health care, and nutrition to low-income children transitioning from preschool to elementary school. This was key to making sure that low-income children didn't fall behind their higher-income peers.

Vivian Malone

On May 30, 1965, Vivian Malone became the first African American to graduate from the University of Alabama. Just two years earlier, Governor George Wallace had tried to personally stop her from registering and the university from integrating at an event called the Stand in the Schoolhouse Door. It would take an order from President John F. Kennedy and the National Guard to force Wallace to back down. Malone went on to join the civil rights division of the U.S. Department of Justice and was present at the signing of the Voting Rights Act of 1965.

Vivian Malone, the first African American to graduate from the University of Alabama.

Freedom schools helped enrich the education of Black children and poor white children.

Freedom Summer in Arkansas

In the summer of 1965, after his successful march of 3,000 students through the streets of Philadelphia, activist Michael Simmons was hard at work on another campaign, called Freedom Summer in Arkansas. He had left school to work for SNCC and recruited 50 volunteers to register hundreds of new voters in Arkansas. But they didn't stop there. Many of the programs that had been effective a year earlier during the Freedom Summer in Mississippi were put in place. The **initiative** opened community centers and started cultural programs, in addition to Freedom Schools.

Freedom Schools taught hundreds of students everything they needed to be politically active citizens who could make a real difference in their communities. They learned about Black history and current events. They learned about segregation and what they could do to end it. These schools educated the next generation of organizers, activists, and lawyers determined to fight for equality.

The following year, students inspired by and trained during Arkansas Freedom Summer would launch a strike to end the segregation of public schools in the nearby town of Marvell. And they would triumph.

Chicago Freedom Movement

As students in the Deep South worked hard during the 1965 Freedom Summer, Dr. King launched a new movement in the Midwest,

King leads thousands of marchers to demonstrate for integrated education in Chicago, Illinois, on July 26, 1965.

called the Chicago Freedom Movement. On July 26, he led a peaceful demonstration of 10,000 people through downtown Chicago.

The march in Chicago called for the government to desegregate public education and end housing and employment discrimination in the city. Chicago was one of the most segregated cities in the United States. White property owners were determined to keep it that way. They did not want African Americans to own homes in nice neighborhoods. They denied them bank loans, physically intimidated them, and banned them from many white middle-class neighborhoods. As a result, Black Americans were forced into low-income housing attached to poor school districts, unable to provide their children with quality public education or a decent standard of living.

Members of the Chicago Freedom Movement, also known as the Chicago Open Housing Movement, demand equal housing rights in Chicago in 1966.

As part of the Freedom Movement, Chicago residents called for "open housing"—the right to purchase homes anywhere, regardless of the buyer's race. Open housing would allow Black residents access to better living situations, job prospects, and schools.

Steps toward Equal Housing

The march in July was just the first of many demonstrations that Dr. King planned as part of the Chicago Freedom Movement. Over the next year, activists rallied in front of real estate offices known for racist policies. They marched into all-white neighborhoods. They remained peaceful in the face of hostile white mobs who used violence against them.

Finally, in August 1966, representatives of the Chicago Real Estate Board agreed to take steps toward open housing. ∎

John Shaw

By the summer of 1965, the civil rights movement's focus on the war in Vietnam had not let up. When 23-year-old John Shaw, a resident of McComb, Mississippi, and beloved friend to many, was killed in action, a wave of anger and sadness went through his community.

Mourning the death of their former high school classmate, local activists in McComb knew that Shaw's death would not be the last if this bloody war continued. It wasn't fair for Black men to be forced to fight and die for the United States when America continually denied them basic civil rights.

The Mississippi Freedom Democratic Party printed a leaflet in its newsletter on July 28, making it the first civil rights organization to issue an official statement against the Vietnam War.

"The WAR ON Viet Nam"

Here are five reasons why Negroes should not be in any War fighting for America:

1. No Mississippi Negroes should be fighting in Viet Nam for the White Mans freedom, until all the Negro People are free in Mississippi

2. Negro boys should not honor the draft here in Mississippi. Mothers should encourage their sons not to go.

3. We will gain respect and dignity as a race only by forcing the United States Government and the Mississippi Government to come with guns, dogs and trucks to take our sons away to fight and be killed protecting Miss, Ala, Ga, and La.

4. No one has a right to ask us to risk our lives and kill other Colored People in Santo Domingo and Viet Nam, so that the White American can get richer. We will be looked upon as traitors by all the Colored People of the world if the Negro people continue to fight and die without a cause.

5. Last week a white soldier from New Jersey was discharged from the Army because he refused to fight in Viet Nam he went on a hunger strike. Negro boys can do the same thing. We can write and ask our sons if they know what they are fighting for. If he answers Freedom, tell him thats what we are fighting for here in Mississippi. And if he says Democracy tell him the truth --- we don't know anything about Communism, Socialism, and all that, but we do know that Negroes have caught hell here under this American Democracy.

- - - - - - - - - - - - - - - - - - - -

This leaflet was passed out and posted in McComb, Mississippi in July 1965. It was written by a group of Negroes in the community who met together after learning a classmate of theirs, John D. Shaw, had been killed in action in Vietnam. Shaw, who was 23 years old, had participated in the 1961 demonstrations in McComb.)

A leaflet protests the Vietnam War.

An elderly Black woman holds a sample voting ballot during a class for newly registered voters in Alabama in 1965.

PERRY COUNTY CIVIC LEAGUE

( ) IRA D. PRUITT
( ) ALBERT TURNER

For Member of the House of Representatives
27th District—Place No. 2—Vote for One

( ) VAN BUREN DANIEL
( ) RICHARD S. MANLEY
( ) F. N. NIXON

For Member State Democratic Executive
Committee—Place No. 1—Old Sixth Congressional District—Vote for One

( ) BRUCE JONES
( ) R. M. (BOB) TUCKER

For Member State Democratic Executive
Committee—Place No. 3—Old Sixth
Congressional District—Vote for One

( ) WILLIAM E. JOHNSTON
( ) W. C. WARREN

For Member State Democratic Executive Committee—Place No. 4—Old Sixth Congressional District—Vote for One.

( ) ALLEN HARGROVE
( ) W. TRUMAN THRASH

For Member State Democratic Executive Committee—Place No. 6—Old Sixth Congressional District. Vote for One.

( ) WILLIAM BANKHEAD McGUIRE
( ) FRANCIS W. SPEAKS

For Member State Democratic Executive Committee—Place No. 6—Old Sixth Congressional District. Vote for One

( ) GERALD E. COLSON
( ) WILLIS E. OAKES

For Sheriff—Vote for One

( ) PATT J. DAVIS
( ) W. U. LOFTIS
( ) ELMER H. NICHOLS
( ) JADIE H. TERRY

For Tax Collector—Vote for One

( ) CHARLES R. JONES
( ) OBIE LEONARD SCOTT
( ) PAUL H. STONE

For Member, Court of County Commissioners,
Uniontown Road District—Place No. 2.
Vote for One

( ) ISOM ATKINS
( ) T. F. (TOM) BOOZER
( ) ROBERT W. (BOBBY) DeVAMPERT

For Member, Court of County Commissioners,
North Perry Road District, Place No. 4.
Vote for One

( ) NORMAN R. CRAWFORD
( ) WILLIE LESTER MARTIN
( ) W. T. RINEHART

For Member, County Board of Education,
Place No. 1. Vote for One

( ) LIONA LANGFORD
( ) P. M. SUTTLE

For Member, County Board of Education,
Place No. 3. Vote for One

( ) A. M. HAYDEN
( ) CLARENCE L. MILLING, JR.

For Member, County Democratic Executive
Committee—Marion Beat 1, Place No. 2
Vote for One

( ) LUCY P. FOSTER
( ) E. HORNE

County Democratic Executive
Oldtown Beat 7, Place No. 1

BURN

5

The Ballot Is Won

In the 1950s, activists made small gains in the
fight for voter rights. The Civil Rights Act of
1957 and the Civil Rights Act of 1960 gave the
federal government slightly more power to
intervene. However, local officials in the South
simply refused to cooperate. Alabama, Arkansas,
Mississippi, Texas, and Virginia still charged poll
taxes that kept many Black people from voting.

The Twenty-Fourth Amendment, ratified in
1964, outlawed poll taxes for federal elections.
Many legislators felt it was incomplete. It did not
prevent states from requiring poll taxes for *local*
elections, which still kept lower-income people
from registering. As a result, they couldn't vote
for local officials like mayor and sheriff—the
officials who affected their lives on a daily basis.
This ban kept most people powerless in their
own communities.

President Johnson (far left) and Dr. King (center) celebrate the Voting Rights Act of 1965.

Voting Rights Act of 1965

In August 1965, three long months after Johnson first introduced Voting Rights legislation, Congress finally approved the bill, and Johnson signed it into law on August 6.

The bill outlawed literacy tests. It also allowed the U.S. attorney general to take action against poll taxes in state and local elections. This ensured that people of all income levels could afford to vote.

Finally, the federal government could intervene in voter registration in any county where less than 50 percent of citizens were registered to vote. The government could send in troops and establish special committees to make sure the registration process was legal and ran smoothly.

Julian Bond

After the passage of the Civil Rights Act of 1964, SNCC activist Julian Bond became one of eleven African Americans elected to the Georgia House of Representatives in 1965.

Bond used his platform to speak out against the Vietnam War. Because of his views, the legislature refused to swear him in as a representative even though he'd been rightfully elected by Atlanta voters. Bond's case eventually reached the U.S. Supreme Court. The justices ruled unanimously that Bond's rights had been violated and he was sworn in as a member of the Georgia House of Representatives.

Julian Bond (center), an African American civil rights worker, was denied a seat in the Georgia House of Representatives because of his criticism of U.S. involvement in Vietnam.

The Thirteenth Amendment

In 1865, after the Civil War was over, the U.S. government passed the Thirteenth Amendment to the U.S. Constitution to abolish slavery. The U.S. Constitution, approved in 1788, is the document that established the framework of government and basic laws of the United States. An amendment is an addition or change added to the original document. The Thirteenth Amendment marked the first time the U.S. Constitution explicitly mentioned slavery.

Abraham Lincoln's 1863 Emancipation Proclamation had announced that all enslaved people in the Confederacy,

Harry and Eliza Stephens of Crawfordsville, Georgia, and their five children survived slavery and the Civil War. They are pictured here in the summer of 1866.

the group of states that had seceded from the Union, would be freed. However, it wasn't until the Thirteenth Amendment passed that this law applied to the entire United States, not just the Confederacy.

The passage of the Thirteenth Amendment marked the beginning of the Reconstruction Era, where the U.S. government introduced a series of laws and amendments designed to grant more rights and freedoms to formerly enslaved people. In 1868, the Fourteenth Amendment granted citizenship to everyone born in the United States, including formerly enslaved people. In 1870, the Fifteenth Amendment declared that the right of citizens to vote should not be denied based on race, color, or if someone was previously enslaved. However, women of all races would have to wait until the Nineteenth Amendment was passed to get the right to vote.

Celebrations in Selma

On August 14, 1965, the first federal voting examiners traveled to Selma to enforce the Voting Rights Act. There, they registered 381 Black voters in a single day—more than they had been able to register in the entire Dallas County in 65 years.

The numbers of registered Black voters climbed steadily. By March 1966, almost 11,000 African Americans had been registered in Selma alone. Remembering the horrors of Bloody Sunday, they swiftly voted Jim Clark out of the sheriff's office. He would never hold public office again.

Annie Maude Williams proudly holds her certificate of eligibility to vote after registering in Selma, Alabama, on August 10, 1965.

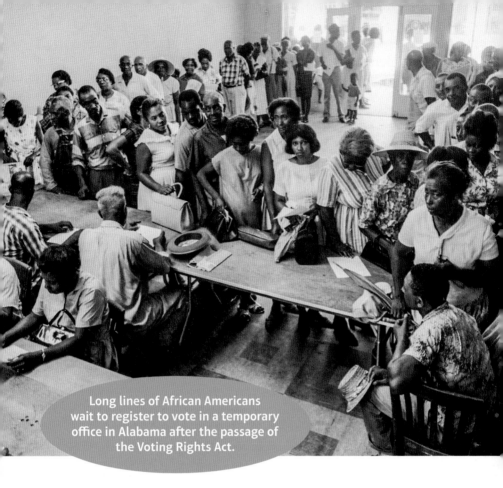

Long lines of African Americans wait to register to vote in a temporary office in Alabama after the passage of the Voting Rights Act.

A New Government

The effect of Black voters was immediately seen in governments across the country, particularly in the Deep South.

In 1965, 250,000 African American voters registered for the first time. In districts where the Voting Rights Act required federal voting examiners to take charge, registration rose even higher. Before the act, only 29.3 percent of African Americans were registered in these districts; after the act, the number jumped to 52.1 percent.

In 9 out of 13 southern states, more than half of all eligible African Americans finally registered successfully.

With more African Americans at the ballot box, Black voters began to elect Black representatives, whom they trusted to look out for their communities' best interests. Within the 11 former Confederate States, the number of African American state

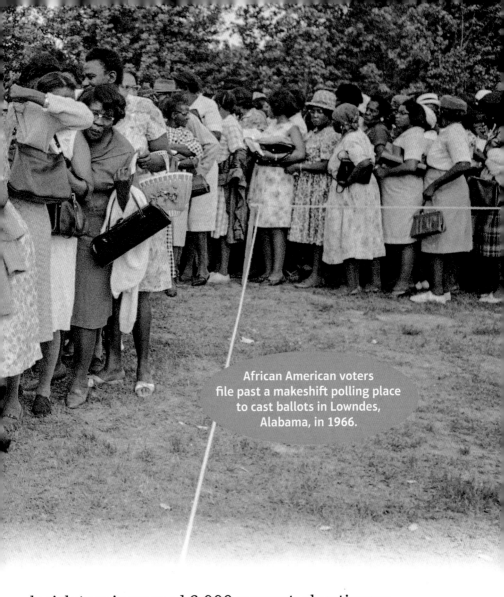

African American voters file past a makeshift polling place to cast ballots in Lowndes, Alabama, in 1966.

legislators increased 6,000 percent, shooting up from 3 to 176 within two decades. In 1965, the states affected by the Voting Rights Act could count only 72 Black elected officials in total. Within 10 years that number would climb to nearly 1,000.

African Americans in elected positions strove to give back to their communities. They not only passed civil rights legislation but also boosted employment.

Fannie Lou Hamer

Fannie Lou Hamer was an activist and SNCC organizer. She helped found the racially integrated Mississippi Freedom Democratic Party (MFDP) as a response to the state's all-white Democratic Party. Just two years earlier, she had been denied the right to register to vote in Indianola, Mississippi. The MFDP registered 80,000 people within a year; the party was especially important because African Americans and people of color made up 42 percent of Mississippi's population.

In 1965, Hamer led members of the party to Washington, DC, to protest voting inequality in the Deep South. The protest she organized there showed members of Congress from all across the country just how dire the situation in Mississippi was. As in Alabama, racism and voter suppression silenced the voices of African American citizens.

When Fannie Lou Hamer attempted to register to vote, she was fired from her job and spent several days in hiding from the KKK.

Blagden Avenue in Washington, DC, was a bustling African American business district in the 1960s.

For decades, cities had awarded valuable contracts to white-owned companies, leaving minority-owned companies scrambling for less just to stay in business. Now the elected officials looked at qualifications, not race. They granted thousands of city contracts to hundreds of minority-owned companies. ■

Children play together in the Watts neighborhood of Los Angeles in 1960.

6

The Push for Housing Equality

The Chicago Freedom Movement had pushed for fairer housing laws. But unequal housing wasn't just a Chicago problem. Across the entire country, racial minorities found themselves crammed into crumbling parts of different cities. African Americans were denied housing loans to move into wealthier areas and struggled to afford soaring housing prices. On top of that, a century of employment discrimination had kept unemployment rates and wages low for African American workers.

President Johnson hoped to change that. On August 10, 1965, he signed into law the Housing and Urban Development Act. This law provided a wide range of payment programs in order to help low-income families purchase decent housing.

It also provided money to citizens in low-income "urban renewal areas" so they could afford to renovate and repair their existing property.

Los Angeles, California

Although these gains were significant, this law alone was not enough to undo the effects of centuries of racial discrimination.

This was particularly the case in Watts, a low-income neighborhood bordering wealthier sections of Los Angeles, California. The mostly Black population in Watts received far fewer social and economic opportunities than their white counterparts, who lived in areas of the city that were

Young people in the Watts neighborhood of Los Angeles were deprived of public spaces and parks that were well kept.

Children in the Watts neighborhood lived amongst lots filled with junk and debris.

off-limits to racial minorities. In Watts, unemployment was extremely high, the quality of public education was extremely low, and living conditions were terrible.

Watts residents had severely limited access to affordable, quality health-care services and reliable public transportation. They were paying taxes just like the white residents in other neighborhoods. Watts residents knew this was unfair. It was only a matter of time before they started standing up for what was right.

Black youth in Watts were often subjected to intimidation and interrogation by Los Angeles police.

Police Brutality in California

Black Americans in California also had another thing to fear: brutality at the hands of the police.

In the 1960s, police patrolled low-income neighborhoods like soldiers. As antiwar protests and civil rights demonstrations became more frequent across the city, the Los Angeles Police Department (LAPD) became more militarized. Police officers armed themselves with weapons, trooped aggressively through minority neighborhoods, and treated many innocent people of color like criminals, often using violence against them.

The LAPD believed minority groups needed to be controlled. Police frequently targeted, beat, and even killed Black and Latino people in order to maintain this illusion of power and control.

An armed police officer searches a man in the Watts neighborhood of Los Angeles in August 1965.

The Watts Uprising

On August 11, 1965, tension between the Black community and police came to a head. A police officer pulled over a 21-year-old African American named Marquette Frye who, the officer claimed, was driving recklessly near his home. When Frye realized he was being arrested, he panicked and began to struggle with the officer. The situation escalated quickly into violence as another enraged officer pulled out a shotgun and used physical force to wrestle Frye to the ground.

Frye's family rushed to his side. Soon, other Watts residents joined them, loudly protesting the brutality. Police arrested Frye, his mother, and his brother. However, the crowd of Watts residents continued to grow even after Frye and his family were taken away.

The arrest of 21-year-old Marquette Frye triggered the August 1965 Watts uprising.

Riots in Watts resulting in store break-ins and theft as mobs of angry protesters took to the streets.

Within hours, thousands of residents were fighting back against decades of discrimination. As a growing army of police officers swarmed to the scene, residents did all that they could to resist police brutality.

Los Angeles Chief of Police William Parker called in 14,000 California National Guard troops. Over the next six days, the protests grew, spreading from Watts all the way south to San Diego, 120 miles away. Day and night, protesters marched through the streets as police took up arms against them. To oppose unfair housing, some protesters burned down buildings.

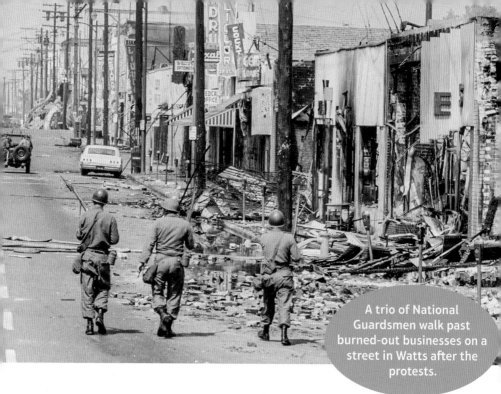

A trio of National Guardsmen walk past burned-out businesses on a street in Watts after the protests.

Between 31,000 and 35,000 adults participated in the protests. In less than a week, 34 people were killed, 1,032 people were injured, and there was $40 million in property damage. The police arrested 3,438 people and beat countless more.

The Push for Fair Housing

As Californians pushed against unfair housing, President Johnson examined the income inequality that led to it.

On September 24, 1965, Johnson signed Executive Order 11246. Instead of simply banning discrimination, this order *required* all companies working for the government to hire employees regardless of race, religion, gender, or national origin.

Operation Hump

On November 8, 1965, the United States launched Operation Hump, an attack against communist Vietnamese fighters. Medic Lawrence Joel received the U.S. Medal of Honor for saving countless lives on the battlefield during an operation. He was the first living African American man since the Spanish-American War of 1898 to receive this medal.

Lawrence Joel (right), with his family, wearing his Medal of Honor.

Women in Civil Rights

In November 1965, Fannie Lou Hamer ran for Congress in Mississippi. Although she lost, she represented one of countless strong female figures powering the civil rights movement. Although they did not always receive the national recognition that leaders like Dr. King did, African American women played a vital role in the ongoing movement.

Ella Baker advised prominent Black thinkers like Thurgood Marshall, W. E. B. Du Bois, Rosa Parks, and even King himself. She cofounded SNCC as an activist organization along with Diane Nash, a leader of the Nashville Student Movement and a Freedom Rider.

Meanwhile, Daisy Bates was the powerhouse behind the Little Rock Nine, the first Black students to integrate an all-white high school in Little Rock, Arkansas. She used a newspaper she had founded, the *Arkansas Weekly*, to call for civil rights.

Septima Poinsette Clark, often called the "Mother of the Movement," opened citizenship schools and created literacy programs to help African Americans register to vote.

Septima Clark holds a plaque awarded to her by the Southern Christian Leadership Conference in 1970.

Dr. King (center) in a news conference discussing the ways in which Chicago mayor Richard Daley could help the Black community.

Meanwhile, the Chicago Freedom Movement soldiered on. In October 1965, SCLC leader James Bevel drummed up support by planning grassroots seminars around the city. And Dr. King urged the movement's members to keep marching forward. "If we can break the system in Chicago," he said, "it can be broken in any place in the country."

The uprising in Watts called national attention to housing inequality. With the eyes of the entire country suddenly trained on the government officials in California, they could no longer ignore the problem. The California Supreme Court reinstated the California Fair Housing Act, which prohibited racial discrimination when renting or selling property, in 1966. ■

Black Panther Party leader Fred Hampton speaks with schoolchildren during a free breakfast program hosted by his organization at a community center in Chicago.

The Legacy of 1965 in Civil Rights History

During the year 1965, Black activists and ordinary citizens alike endured brutal violence in their fight for civil rights. The death of Jimmie Lee Jackson at a peaceful prayer vigil inspired the historic Selma to Montgomery March, a turning point in the year. The nation watched on TV as men and women marching across the Edmund Pettus Bridge were beaten to the ground by law enforcement, and a wave of public support for equal rights for Black people rose up. The Voting Rights Act of 1965 drastically increased African Americans' ability to register and vote. The struggle for access to quality affordable housing and good schools continued. However, in the months and years ahead, there would still be more violence and bloodshed.

On October 15, 1966, bold young organizers founded the Black Panther Party in Oakland, California. The Panthers served food to thousands of low-income children every day. They also monitored police violence to hold police accountable for brutality, and they opened a school.

Tragedy struck on April 4, 1968, when Martin Luther King, Jr. was assassinated while supporting a sanitation workers' strike in Memphis, Tennessee. Heartbroken, thousands of Americans in more than 100 cities took to the streets to protest his death.

The body of Dr. Martin Luther King, Jr., and thousands of his supporters make their way through the streets to Morehouse College in Atlanta, Georgia, for a memorial service.

President Johnson signs the Civil Rights Act of 1968 into law in a White House ceremony.

In response to the public protests, President Johnson finally signed the Civil Rights Act of 1968 (also known as the Fair Housing Act of 1968) on April 11. This further strengthened the power of the federal government to intervene to protect citizens, which was especially important in southern states where racist local officials often refused—sometimes violently—to uphold civil rights legislation.

However, in practice, **defacto** segregation remains common in many areas of the country.

In 2013, the Supreme Court case *Shelby County v. Holder* struck down most of the 1965 Voting Rights Act. The Court's decision no longer allows the federal government to run and oversee elections in nine southern states. As a result, many polling places in these states closed; most of them were in counties with many African American residents, making it more difficult for them to vote. Today, the fight for voting rights for Black Americans is as threatened as ever.

The legacy of 1965 lives on in modern movements such as Black Lives Matter, which fights for racial justice and an end to police brutality.

Members of the WNBA Indiana Fever show their support for Black Lives Matter before a game in 2020.

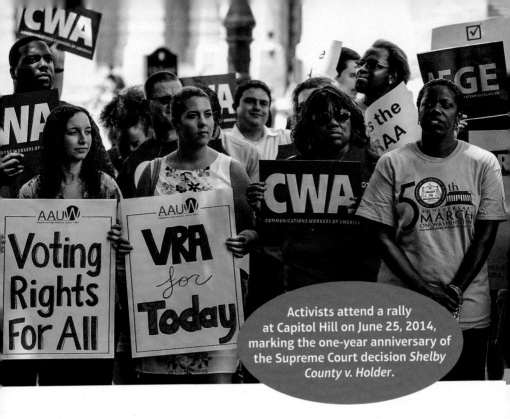

Activists attend a rally at Capitol Hill on June 25, 2014, marking the one-year anniversary of the Supreme Court decision *Shelby County v. Holder*.

Just as in the 1960s, racial minorities have many protections on paper, but those do not always translate to equality in real life. Today, Black people are still more likely than white people to be murdered by the police. The Black unemployment rate is twice as high as it is for white people. Black men and women also typically earn less money than their white counterparts.

The fight for civil rights is far from over. But the key to victory is the same now as it was during the original civil rights movement: unity. When everyone joins together to fight for good, then the world can change, and America can finally become a country with true equality for all. ∎

Kamala Harris

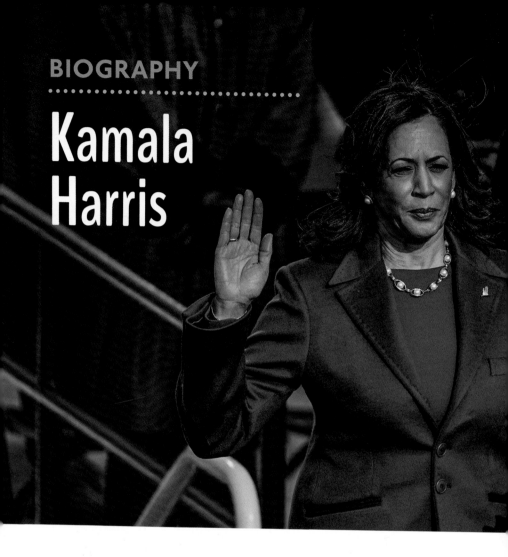

Vice President Kamala Harris was born on October 20, 1964, just months after the passage of the Civil Rights Act of 1964.

Harris has spent her life working for justice within the legal system and the U.S. government.

She learned the importance of racial integration and diversity as a child growing up in a biracial household. Both of her parents were immigrants: her father was Jamaican of African descent, and her mother was Indian. She was born in Oakland, California, the same city

Kamala Harris takes the vice presidential oath of office in Washington, DC, on January 20, 2021.

where the Black Panther Party was founded in 1966.

Although raised in the United States, the young Harris often spent time with her family in India. Her Indian grandfather, a **civil servant**, was one of her greatest role models. He fiercely believed in civil rights and in democracy—and he taught her to do the same.

After attending the historically Black Howard University, Harris went to law school and became the first woman elected as a San Francisco district attorney in 2003. As a district attorney, she routinely took a firm stance against

One-year-old Kamala poses with her mother, Shymala Gopalan Harris.

policies that she saw as unjust. She publicly opposed the death penalty, which disproportionately targets African Americans. At least 4 percent of people on death row are estimated to be innocent.

In 2011, Harris became the first female and first African American attorney general of California. She used her position to work for LGBTQ rights and helped

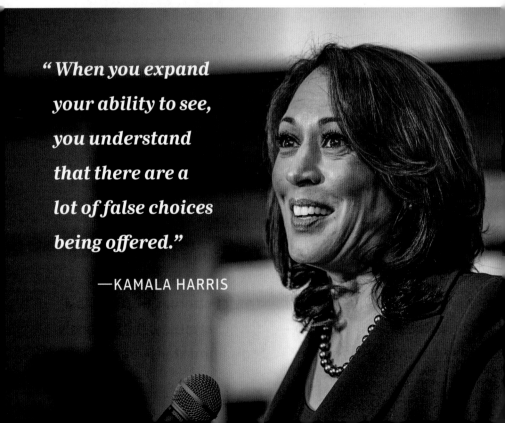

"*When you expand your ability to see, you understand that there are a lot of false choices being offered.*"

—KAMALA HARRIS

pave the way to marriage equality across the United States in 2015.

Additionally, she tried to reduce police brutality in California by introducing special training for police officers that promoted racial equality. Under her direction, the California Department of Justice became the first state agency to require police officers to wear body cameras. Body cameras help ensure that officers are monitored and can be held accountable for committing police brutality.

Kamala Harris in 2006 when she was the San Francisco district attorney.

When Harris was elected to the U.S. Senate in 2016, representing California, she became the first Indian American to be a U.S. senator. She was also only the second African American woman in history to hold this position.

As a senator, she focused on improving immigration and criminal justice policies, raising the minimum wage, and helping women access health care options.

In November 2020, Kamala Harris made history as the first woman, the first African American, and the first person of South Asian descent to be elected as vice president of the United States, when she ran alongside President Joe Biden.

TIMELINE

The Year in Civil Rights

1965

JANUARY 2

SNCC announces that it will focus on increasing Black voter registration in Dallas County, Alabama.

JANUARY 4

President Lyndon B. Johnson announces the Great Society initiative.

FEBRUARY 18

State troopers in Alabama kill Jimmie Lee Jackson.

FEBRUARY 21

Malcolm X is assassinated in the Audubon Ballroom in New York City.

MARCH 7

Police beat hundreds of peaceful protesters on Bloody Sunday in Jacksonville, Florida.

MARCH 9

During the second march to Montgomery, Dr. King turns protesters around on the Edmund Pettus Bridge.

MARCH 21

The march from Selma to Montgomery attracts 25,000 participants.

APRIL 11

President Johnson signs the Elementary and Secondary Education Act of 1965.

JULY

Freedom Summer in Arkansas educates hundreds of future organizers in the Deep South.

JULY 26

King leads a march of 10,000 members of the Chicago Freedom Movement.

AUGUST 6

President Johnson signs the Voting Rights Act of 1965 into law.

AUGUST 11

The Watts uprising in California continues for six days and nights.

SEPTEMBER 24

President Johnson signs Executive Order 11246 to end employment discrimination.

NOVEMBER 8

U.S. launches Operation Hump, after which Lawrence Joel receives the Medal of Honor.

NOVEMBER

Fannie Lou Hamer challenges the seating of elected congressmen from Mississippi.

GLOSSARY

activist (AK-tiv-ist) a person who works to bring about political or social change

apartheid (uh-PAAR-tide) in South Africa, a policy and system of segregation and discrimination on grounds of race

assassination (uh-sas-uh-NAY-shun) the murder of someone well-known or important

civil rights (SIV-uhl rites) the individual rights that all members of a democratic society have to freedom and equal treatment under the law

civil servant (SIV-uhl SUR-vuhnt) a person who works for the government

communism (KAHM-yuh-niz-uhm) a way of organizing the economy of a country so that all the resources and businesses belong to the government, and the profits are shared by all

defacto (DEE-fak-toe) in fact, or in effect, by right or not

deputize (DEP-yuh-tyz) to appoint someone to be a type of law enforcement officer

discrimination (dis-krim-uh-NAY-shuhn) prejudice or unfair behavior to others based on differences in such things as race, gender, or age

federal (FED-ur-uhl) national government, as opposed to state or local government

initiative (i-NISH-uh-tiv) the ability to take action without being told what to do

integration (in-tuh-GRAY-shuhn) the practice of uniting people from different races in an attempt to give people equal rights

Jim Crow (jim kro) the former practice of segregating Black people in the United States

Ku Klux Klan (KOO klux KLAN) a secret organization in the United States that uses threats and violence to achieve its goal of white supremacy; also called the Klan or the KKK

legislation (lej-is-LAY-shuhn) laws that have been proposed or made

liberation (lib-uh-RAY-shuhn) the act of breaking free from oppression

low-income (loh IN-kuhm) when a person or family earns or receives a small amount of money, especially from working

lynching (LIN-ching) a sometimes public murder by a group of people, often involving hanging

Nation of Islam (NAY-shun ov iz-LAHM) an African American movement and organization that combines the religion of Islam with Black nationalist ideas

National Guard (NASH-uh-nuhl gahrd) a volunteer military organization with units in each state that are commanded by the governor and president

nonviolent resistance (non-VYE-uh-luhnt ri-ZIS-tuhns) the pursuit of social change through peaceful political actions

oppression (uh-PRESH-uhn) cruel and unjust treatment of a group of people

poll tax (pohl taks) a tax of a fixed amount per person placed on adults and often linked to the right to vote

segregation (seg-ruh-GAY-shuhn) the act or practice of keeping people or groups apart

suffrage (SUHF-rij) the right to vote

voter suppression (VOH-tur suh-PRESH-uhn) preventing a certain group of people from being able to vote

white supremacist (wite su-PREM-uh-sist) a person who believes that the white race is better than other races and that white people should have control over people of other races

BIBLIOGRAPHY

"Anti-Draft Movement." *SNCC Digital Gateway*, July 14, 2020, snccdigital.org/events/anti-draft-movement

Brockell, Gillian. "William F. Buckley Jr. vs. James Baldwin: A Racial Showdown on the American Dream." *Washington Post*, August 13, 2020, washingtonpost.com/history/2019/09/15/william-f-buckley-jr-vs-james-baldwin-racial-showdown-american-dream/

Harmon, Rick. "Timeline: The Selma-to-Montgomery Marches." *USA Today*, March 6, 2015, usatoday.com/story/news/nation/2015/03/05/black-history-bloody-sunday-timeline/24463923/

"History of the Voting Rights Act." *American Civil Liberties Union*, September 12, 2017, aclu.org/issues/voting-rights/voting-rights-act/history-voting-rights-act

"Major Acts of Congress." *Encyclopedia.com*, January 4, 2021, encyclopedia.com/history/encyclope-dias-almanacs-transcripts-and-maps/housing-and-urban-development-act-1965

Michals, Debra, ed. "Fannie Lou Hamer." *National Women's History Museum*, womenshistory.org/education-resources/biographies/fannie-lou-hamer

The People History—Steve Pearson. "What Happened in 1965
Important News and Events, Key Technology and Popular
Culture." *The People History*, thepeoplehistory.com/1965.html

"Selma Voting Rights Campaign." *SNCC Digital Gateway*, July 14,
2020, snccdigital.org/events/selma-voting-rights-campaign/

Thurow, Aishling, and Anna Lemberger. "7 Women Civil
Rights Leaders You Need to Know." *One*, March 6, 2020,
one.org/us/blog/7-kick-ass-women-civil-rights-leaders-
you-need-to-know/

A crowd gathers in front of the Montgomery capitol building during the Selma to Montgomery march for civil rights, on March 25, 1965.

INDEX

About the Author

Jay Leslie writes about revolutionaries. Her other books include *Who Did It First? 50 Politicians, Activists and Entrepreneurs Who Revolutionized the World* and *Game, Set, Sisters! The Story of Venu and Serena Williams.* Connect with Jay at www.Jay-Leslie.com.

PHOTO CREDITS